The Pilgrim's Progress™

Based on John Bunyan's
epic masterpiece

Steve R Cleary
with Robert Fernandez

Executive Editor: Steve Cleary
Writers: Steve Cleary and Robert Fernandez
Based on the allegory *The Pilgrim's Progress* written by John Bunyan in 1678
Creative Director: Andrea Lyons
Copy Editors: Meredee Berg/Traci McConnell
Images from: The Pilgrim's Progress Animated Movie by Cat in the Mill, LLC
Distributed by RevelaitonMedia [www.RevelationMedia.com]
In partnership with Herald Entertainment [www.Herald-inc.com] and
American Family Association [www.AFA.net]

First Printing 2018
Printed in the United States of America

www.Pilgrims.Movie
#PilgrimsProgressMovie

ISBN: 978-0-9992893-4-1

Dedicated to my precious
granddaughters, Tally and Tatum—
my Shining Ones. I pray you always
journey on the straight path.

John Bunyan

1678

"I saw a man clothed with rags ... a book in his hand and a great burden upon his back."

The Pilgrim's Progress story was written by John Bunyan (1628-1688), one of the most famous preachers in English history. Regarded as a Puritan, he was arrested for "preaching without a license" and imprisoned in a dark, dank cell. Tempted by his captors with the promise of freedom if he would simply refrain from further preaching, Bunyan famously replied, "If you release me today, I shall preach tomorrow." He remained imprisoned for twelve years and there he had a daytime dream about a pilgrim named Christian.

Thus, the greatest work of fiction in the history of the English language began with a simple man, imprisoned for preaching the Good News of salvation, using his time and imagination to record the trials and triumphs of his Christian journey.

Over the past three centuries, this story, written from a prison cell, has taken root in the hearts of adults and children alike. It is an international best seller, (only the Holy Bible has sold more copies) was smuggled to the underground church, and has been translated into more than two hundred languages. For generations, parents have read *The Pilgrim's Progress* to their children, regarding its importance second only to the Holy Bible.

The implicit gift of this extraordinary allegory is that, as we read it, we are given an invaluable view of reality. This reality provides clear insight into all of life—the difficulties, the obstacles, and the suffering, but also the promise of redemption, restoration, and life with the Celestial King in His Celestial City.

There once was a man named Christian who lived in the City of Destruction. Its name in the ancient tongue was Noitcurtsed but its rulers soon set upon the more pleasant name of "Not Cursed." However, some would have thought it wishful thinking, for the city was indeed cursed with perpetual toil and decay.

It was from this city that Christian began a treacherous and dangerous journey from which he would never return.

It was in that cursed city that Christian came upon a book—or as some would later say, perhaps the Book came upon him?

For no sooner had Christian opened the cover, he was unable to pry himself from its entrancing pages. And so he read … and read … and read and read. And the more he read the more his concern for right things grew until this became for him a very great burden.

Christian's wife, **Christiana,** thought her husband had gone mad with his talk of war, fire from the sky, their city's destruction—and of a journey outside the borders to a Celestial City, ruled by a good and noble King.

"It makes no sense at all!" she protested.

"So, you must choose, Christian. Choose between me and the children … or doing as your silly Book says."

"FOR WE WILL NOT GO WITH YOU!"

Once outside the borders, Christian's burden, along with his anxiety, continued to grow. "What shall I do?" he knelt and cried. And when he looked up, he saw a man named **Evangelist** who would serve as his guide.

"Don't wipe away your tears, look through them. Sometimes tears have a way of bringing clarity."

"Now, don't hesitate. Don't waste any more time! Do what you know you must! You'll soon see with your eyes what you believe in your heart and you'll be rid of that burden on your back!"

Two acquaintances from the City of Destruction tried to stop Christian on his journey and bring him back home. Though very persuasive, **Obstinate** and **Pliable's** arguments could not extinguish Christian's steadfast determination.

"That Book, which you should never have read in the first place, has done nothing but set you on a journey for a hope and a dream that does not exist! Don't be a fool, Christian. Think of your family!" pleaded Obstinate.

His appeals ignored, Obstinate returned to the city. But Pliable, inspired by talk of the Celestial City, continued on with Christian.

Eager to reach their destination, Pliable grabbed Christian by the arm and ran as fast as he could, only to find they were falling headlong into a swamp—the **Swamp of Despondency**.

The swamp was filled with the slime, muck, and mire of men's fears. It was where many gave up their journey, though they had barely started.

"If this is what it's like to follow you in the beginning," shouted Pliable, "how could it possibly be any better in the end? So much for your book! I have no problem changing MY mind. No, sir, no problem whatsoever!"

So Pliable abandoned his helpless friend to the swamp and, following in the footsteps of his friend Obstinate, made his way back to the City of Destruction.

With his burden too heavy to stay afloat, Christian began sinking deeper and deeper into the mud. Just as he was going under, he cried out with his last breath,

"HELP!"

From what seemed like out of nowhere, a response came, "You called?" Help answered and lifted the slime-covered pilgrim onto the bank.

"This journey you're embarking on is not for the double-minded! No, no. Not for the wishy-washy. Not at all! And this swamp, it's nothing compared to the trouble that's ahead. *Endurance comes before the prize,*' the Book says."

"And remember, Help, in some form or another, is never far away."

Christian, alone and unsure, proceeded on his journey. He then encountered a "wise man" who persuaded him that there was an easier path than that which he was on—and that continuing on his current path was not only unnecessary, but unwise as well. He convinced Christian to take an easier path to a village named **Morality** with the promise of being relieved of his dreadful burden.

"Worldly's the name. **Worldly** first, **Wiseman** last, of course—and don't ever mix them up! Now, what was this Evangelist thinking, sending you in this direction, which is full of nothing but trouble and danger, which I can see by the scratches and the mud you have already experienced! No, don't continue this way, which is silly nonsense, but go that other way which is not."

Upon arriving in Morality, Christian was told that if he wanted to rid himself of his burden, he must climb a hill where he would encounter a man made of stone—whose name was **Mr. Legality.**

The hill was covered with commandments, etched in stone, each with a specific instruction, each one different from the last.

"You wretched, wretched man! You expect me to help you when you cannot even help yourself! Keep trying to make your way up here! Keep trying! You must follow ALL of the instructions! ALL of them, I say!" Mr. Legality commanded.

Unable to obey all the commandments and climb the mountain, Christian fell under their heavy weight. Once again, Evangelist came to his aid and instructed him, "Follow the Light to that wooden gate. There you shall be told what to do."

Trouble was, before arriving at that place, Christian was surrounded by flying demons who had been sent by their master to prevent the pilgrim from venturing further.

Narrowly escaping the demons' attack and making his way through the gate, Christian thought his journey was finally over. But the Gatekeeper advised him that was not the case.

"You think your journey's over? Oh no, dear boy. Your journey is just beginning. And if I were you, I'd make a dash for it right about now!"

Seeing a swarm of demons flying towards him, Christian ran as the Gatekeeper stayed back to thwart the attack!

After scarcely escaping the demons' assault, Christian was led to the house of the Interpreter—a being of pure light who instructed him on how to find his way in the darkness that was soon to overtake him.

"Things are not always as they seem, dear Christian. And sometimes life's tumbles lead us to the most interesting places."

"You must look and not just see. You must listen and not just hear."

The Interpreter also showed Christian an **Old Man in a Cage,** whose only words were …

"NO HOPE! NO HOPE! NOOO HOPE!"

Christian was puzzled as to who this man was and why he was locked in a cage. The answer to that question, and many others, he would soon discover.

esuming his journey, Christian came to a fork in the road. There were two signs, each pointing a different way.

PATIENCE PATH:
A path full of rocks—narrow and steep.

PASSION PASSAGE:
Stretching over the flatland— pleasant and lush and green.

Christian had learned not to veer off the path after being tempted to choose an easier way. This time, choosing the more difficult upward path, **Patience Path,** Christian persevered through the struggle and reached the top.

It was there that the light of the Cross broke the bindings of his heavy burden. At last Christian was free!

"I'm Free! I'm Free!"

It was at **Salvation Hill** that Christian was converted and transformed. The **Shining Ones** sang with delight and clothed him with new garments for his new life.

"Stepped out alone in sorrowed burden,
faced hardship, heartache, and attack.
Stood firm and learned to see beyond sight,
now not alone you join the fight!

So be refreshed, oh gentle pilgrim,
a pauper prince you have become.
No longer burdened or alone,
that many steps closer to home."

Apollyon was furious with his demons (also known as the **Supervisors**) who were unable to stop Christian on his journey toward the Celestial City. He was even more infuriated that his demons suggested giving up.

"Let him be, you say? LET HIM BE?!" Apollyon angrily shouted at one of his incompetent servants. "The fool is a bigger threat to us now than he ever was before! If he does not give up soon, others will try the same thing!"

"HE MUST BE STOPPED!!!"

ack on the path, Christian continued on his journey. But before nightfall came, he was nearly knocked down by two men running toward him who were overcome with fear of the dangers ahead.

The men, **Fearful** and **Mistrust**, pleaded with Christian to turn back before it was too late!

In the darkness of night, Christian discovered the reason that the two men were running away. Two stone lions, with bright red eyes, had come to life. Each one growled fiercely as Christian came near.

"I have no choice. I must keep going," Christian convinced himself as he lunged forward, barely passing between their massive heads and gaping jaws.

Watchful welcomed the weary pilgrim into his home—The Palace Beautiful—where he and his daughters, DISCRETION, PIETY, CHARITY & PRUDENCE helped prepare Christian for the next phase of his journey.

"You did well, good Christian, and have passed a trial of your faith. Be at peace and lay your burden at the feet of your King, for *not one hair of your head falls without Him knowing.*"

rom prince to warrior, Christian's transformation had begun as Watchful's daughters equipped him with armor of steel and might:

THE HELMET OF SALVATION

THE BREASTPLATE OF RIGHTEOUSNESS

THE SHIELD OF FAITH

THE SWORD OF THE SPIRIT

THE BELT OF TRUTH

FEET SHOD WITH THE GOSPEL OF PEACE

hristian was then led to the Valley of Humiliation, a valley all pilgrims must face—and face alone. It was there that he encountered the temptation of the evil Apollyon, a master of deception, who presented himself … first, as an ordinary, yet very persuasive man.

"I think it is best that you turn back. You would not be the first, you know. Or would you rather lose all that you hold dear for a future that is so uncertain? Come now, good Christian, and put down your sword."

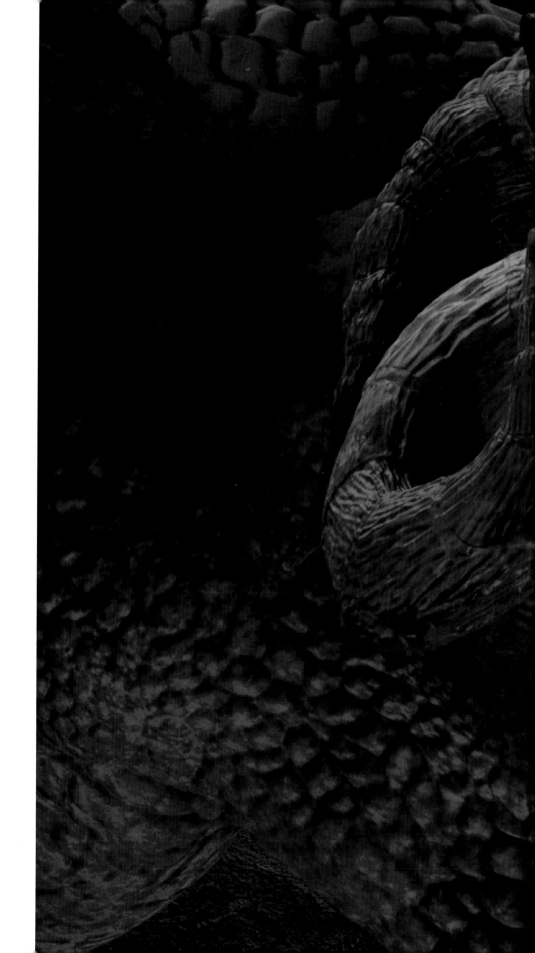

nmoved by the words of Apollyon, Christian raised his sword, for he knew Apollyon was no mere man—rather, he was the Devil himself!

"You deceiver, liar, usurper of all that is good and true! I served under you and found nothing but misery. My allegiance is entirely to the KING!" Christian shouted and stood fast.

With every ounce of his might, Christian bravely fought Apollyon for hours on end. The dragon was ruthless, using all of his powers and rage. Then, just when it seemed defeat was inevitable, Christian swung his sword one last time, plunging it deep into the demon's coarse scales.

"URGH! You will see me again, Christian!" the wounded beast proclaimed. "When the waves overpower you, when death's cold arms wrap themselves around your wretched soul … I will be there!"

"I WILL BE THERE!"

After the great fight with Apollyon, Christian encountered another pilgrim on his quest. His name was **Faithful Pathfinder,** and he had journeyed outside the borders of the City of Destruction shortly before Christian. It was at Faithful Pathfinder's house that Christian first discovered the Book.

Together they happened upon Evangelist once more, who warned them of greater dangers ahead. In a town … or rather, a fair …

Vanity Fair was erected on the path to the Celestial City by the evil Apollyon, Beelzebub, and their Legion. The town hosted a fair that never ceased and that possessed everything that could seduce the human heart.

Upon entering the town, Christian and Faithful Pathfinder were offered every indulgence, every vice that distracts mankind and tempts their worldly desires. Refusing to take part in any of the fair's offerings, they were dragged to the town's justice—Judge Hategood! There the townspeople accused the travelers, of causing a criminal disruption of the ongoing fair.

"What is the meaning of this? What is this massive interruption to our fair? ORDER! ORDER, I SAY, AND CALL THE JURY!"

GUILTY!

THE JURY: Mr. Blindman, Mrs. Nogood, Miss Malice, Mr. Lovelust, Mr. Liveloose, Mrs. Heady, Mr. Highminded, Miss Enmity, Mrs. Liar, Mrs. Hatelight, Mr. Nosatisfying and Mr. Cruelty.

"You offer peace and joy, but *that* you cannot buy. Otherwise it would be for sale here at Vanity Fair. The court finds you guilty, and I sentence you to death!" Judge Hategood declared.

Faithful and Christian had been warned by Evangelist that one or both men would not leave Vanity Fair alive. Faithful was first to receive his sentence of death.

"Do not weep that I am sent ahead of you, dear Brother. Stay true! Stay true, and I shall see you. I shall see you, again."

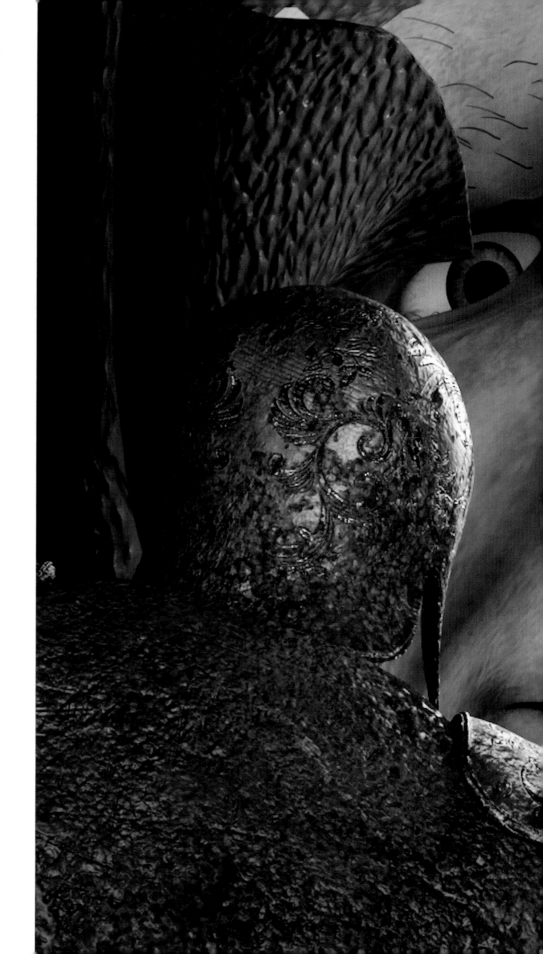

Christian escaped Vanity Fair with the help of one of the town guards—a man by the name of **Hopeful**, who had been inspired by the courageous faith of Christian and Faithful. The two journeyed together until Christian suggested a shortcut through a path much easier to navigate.

Before long, they realized that they were lost and the narrow path was nowhere in sight. As a violent storm approached, they ran for the closest shelter.

Upon waking the next morning, they found themselves as prisoners of **Giant Despair,** for Christian and Hopeful had unwittingly stumbled into his giant-sized boot.

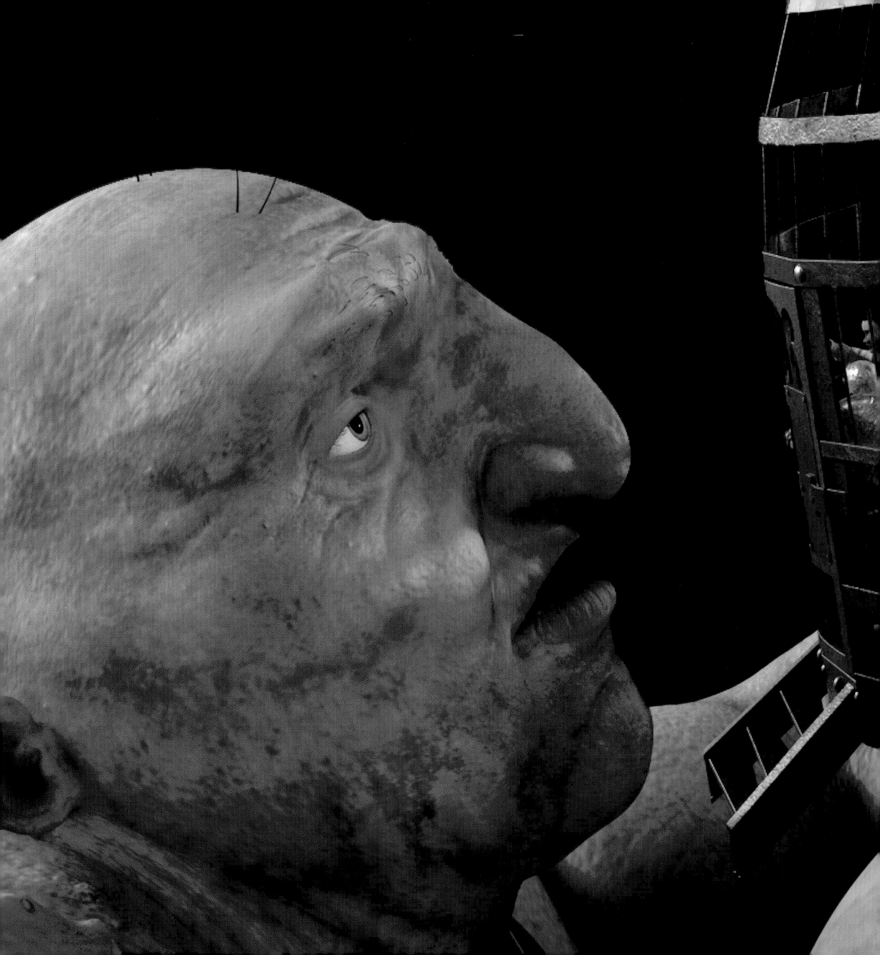

Giant Despair locked Christian and Hopeful in a cage made of steel. Days passed with no food or water and the walls echoed their despair. Christian's hope was waning, and the giant was fuming because his prisoners still refused to take their own lives.

"What?! You're still alive? I gave you everything you needed to do the job!" raged Giant Despair.

Then, with great surprise to Christian and Hopeful, the giant worked himself into a frenzy, until he passed out and fell to the floor with a great thud!

The giant's wife, **Diffidence,**—beautiful in her own eyes—rushed in at the sound and found her husband passed out on the ground. She let out a tirade, that only she could express, when her *lug* of a husband fainted at the slightest hint of stress.

"ARRRR! I should have listened to my mum when she warned me not to marry you, you bungling, good-for-nothing goon! I could've had my pick of any eligible giant, being the beauty I was. But no, I had to pick the pretty one, I did!"

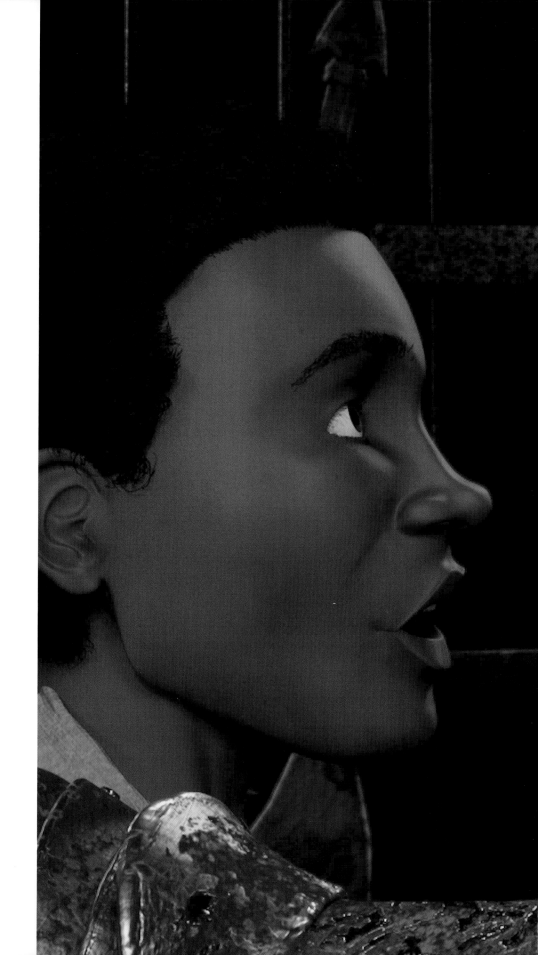

Finally, Hopeful realized for reasons unknown, that the giants were prevented from killing their prisoners. Death came only when a prisoner's despair grew to such magnitude that they took their own life.

It was then that Christian understood; the old man in the cage, shouting "NO HOPE!" was actually himself, with no hope of escape from the dungeon of despair.

As the pilgrims quickly recalled their hope in the great King, a key appeared—a gift from the Interpreter who had explained, "Things are not always as they seem."

After escaping the grasp of Giant Despair, Christian and Hopeful vowed to remain on the straight path, determining not to stray from it again. It was on this path that they met a shepherd named **Knowledge**.

"I give you this map for the rest of your journey," the shepherd said. "Beware the Flatterer. Keep the Light of the City, which reflects that of its Builder, ever before you. The way is safe for whom it is safe, and dangerous for whom it is dangerous. Let this knowledge suffice for now: that you do not walk alone, for the King guides you as a shepherd guides his sheep."

With renewed confidence to complete their journey, the two pilgrims pressed on. They soon met the **Wizard**—who desired to hear all about the great adventures and accomplishments that the two had experienced.

"Your names are Christian and Hopeful? What great names! Surely, they must reflect your good character! I can only imagine the things you have endured to get this far. Please tell me all!"

Christian and Hopeful began to speak of all their quests. The more they recounted their exploits, the more the Wizard flattered them with praise. And the more the Wizard flattered, the more Christian and Hopeful's hearts filled with pride.

It was then that a net sprang up from the ground, wrapped around them, and trapped them in their obvious shame.

Having succeeded with his crafty plan, the Wizard revealed his true identity—a demon in the service of the evil Apollyon.

"Well aren't you the greatest ... the greatest FOOLS, I should say!" exclaimed the Wizard with glee. "Try as you might, you'll never get loose! See these strands? They were woven with your own boasting!"

Eventually, one of the Shining Ones came to aid Christian and Hopeful. After cutting them free, she sternly reminded the pilgrims that they had failed to follow the Shepherd's good map. For it was not a typical map as they thought, but rather a map of instruction with the neglected warning, "Beware the Flatterer."

Freed from the net of pride, Christian and Hopeful made their way to the edge of the **Raging River** where they could see, just on the other side, the light of the Celestial City. The river seethed with power—a towering wall of water reaching up to the sky. Instinctively, they knew they were at the end of their journey.

Hopeful felt faith rise in his heart—so much so, that he leapt into the river and quickly disappeared from Christian's sight. But Christian wavered and thought long and hard, "Do I enter now or return to my family? What about my wife and children? I must go back and save them, while I can."

It was then that his friend Evangelist appeared one more time, explaining that the decision to take this journey must be made by each alone. The King had never failed him, and He would not fail him now.

With renewed confidence and courage, Christian leapt into the Raging River, never to return.

The Journey of Every Christian

The message contained in John Bunyan's classic work *The Pilgrim's Progress* is the journey of every Christian seeking salvation "from this world to that which is to come."

Every day we must choose if we are going to focus our attention on this world, a world that will face judgment and decay, or if we are setting our sights on eternity with our King. Even when we choose to journey on the straight and narrow path, we face constant temptation, distractions, and false teachings that can lead us astray. And those who present themselves as friends may actually be foes.

So, each and every day we must consider carefully the path we will take. Often the right path is the path filled with difficulties and, sometimes, even despair. And though at times we may struggle and fail, our King is there to give help, comfort, and even forgiveness, if we are simply willing to ask.

May this story encourage the Christian (a pilgrim in this world) to continually seek the King and His ways and remain on the straight and narrow path. To those who have not committed their lives to the King, we pray this story will inspire you to consider which world will last.

God's Faithful Pilgrims

They were strangers and pilgrims on this earth …
They desired a better place, a heavenly country …
Where God is not ashamed to be called their God.

They lived by faith even when mistreated …
They gained strength out of weakness …
They refused to deny their King.

And God has prepared an Eternal City for them …
And all of His Pilgrims who journey this same path …
For these are of whom this world is not worthy.

[adapted from Hebrews 11]

*"A man there was, though some did count him
mad, the more he cast away the more he had."*
–John Bunyan, *The Pilgrim's Progress*

RevelationMedia is bringing quality, culturally relevant films free to the global missions' community. Films that promote biblical literacy, discipleship, and world evangelism. Films that reach our children, who live in a media-distracted world, and that break the barriers of engagement in the farthest corners of the earth.

www.RevelationMedia.com